FRRLS-FY JUV
31022005970303
J 598.47 SWAN ERIN
Swan, Erin Pembrey.
Penguins :

1/04

D1416277

Erin Pembrey Swan

Penguins

From Emperors to Macaronis

Franklin Watts - A Division of Scholastic Inc.
New York • Toronto • London • Auckland • Sydney
Mexico City • New Delhi • Hong Kong
Danbury, Connecticut

Photographs © 2003: Animals Animals: 40 (Ken Cole), 37 (K. Westerkov); Dembinsky Photo Assoc.: cover, 21 (Rod Planck), 42 (Ira Rubin), 7 (Mark J. Thomas); Peter Arnold Inc.: 27, 31, 39 (Fred Bruemmer), 25 (David Cavagnaro), 19 (Doug Cheeseman), 43 (Luiz C. Marigo), 1, 5 bottom left (Fritz Polking), 5 top right, 13, 35 (Kevin Schafer), 5 top left, 17 (Roland Seitre), 23 (Tom Vezo), 5 bottom right, 15 (Bruno P. Zehnder), 29 (Gunter Ziesler); Photo Researchers, NY/John Eastcott & Yva Momatiuk: 33; Visuals Unlimited/Gerald & Buff Corsi: 6.

Illustrations by Pedro Julio Gonzalez, Steve Savage, and A. Natacha Pimentel C.

The photo on the cover shows rockhopper penguins. The photo on the title page shows a group of emperor penguin chicks.

Library of Congress Cataloging-in-Publication Data

Swan, Erin Pembrey.
    Penguins: from emperors to macaronis / Erin Pembrey Swan.
    p. cm. – (Animals in order)
    Summary: Describes the general physical characteristics and behavior of penguins and takes an in-depth look at fourteen different species.
    ISBN 0-531-12264-6
    Includes bibliographical references.
    1. Penguins—Juvenile literature. [1. Penguins.] I. Title. II. Series.
QL696.S47 S93 2003
598.47—dc21   2002008886

©2003 Franklin Watts, a division of Scholastic Inc.
All rights reserved. Published simultaneously in Canada.
Printed in the United States of America.
1 2 3 4 5 6 7 8 9 10 R 12 11 10 09 08 07 06 05 04 03

Contents

Meet the Penguins

What comes to mind when you think about penguins?

To many people, penguins are funny, black and white birds that live at the South Pole. This is true of some penguins, but did you know that one kind of penguin lives in the desert? Or that another kind lives in the forest instead of on ice and snow?

All penguins belong to the same group, or order, called the sphenisciformes (SFEN-ih-see-FOR-meez). Despite some differences, including where some of them live, penguins have many things in common. It is the traits they share that place penguins together in the same scientific order.

The four penguins on the next page have many things in common. Can you guess what some of those might be?

Rockhopper penguin

African penguin

Adelie penguin

Emperor penguin

Traits of the Sphenisciformes

One of the most obvious things that penguins have in common is the way they look. All penguins have white fronts and black backs. Penguins catch their food in the ocean, and their coloring helps protect them. When a penguin is swimming, its front is facing the bottom of the ocean and its back is turned up to the sky. If an enemy swims under a penguin and looks up, the penguin's white belly blends in with the bright sky above it. When an enemy swims or flies over a penguin and looks down, the penguin's black back makes it difficult to see against the dark water. A penguin's *camouflage* helps keep it safe from enemies such as seals and sharks.

Penguins are also one of the few birds that cannot fly. They make up for this with their swimming skills. Penguins catch all their food in the water, where there is plenty of fish, squid, and tiny, shrimplike krill to make a meal. When penguins swim, they use their wings as flippers and their tails as rudders

Penguins are excellent swimmers and catch all of their food in the water.

to help them steer. They have wide, flat feet that push them forward and waterproof feathers that keep them dry. Penguins can swim in very cold water. Their dense feathers and the thick layers of blubber under their skin keep them warm and cozy, even in the iciest ocean. Penguins also have special glands near their eyes that *excrete* extra salt from their bodies. With the help of these glands, penguins can drink salt water as well as freshwater. That is a great advantage for birds that live near the ocean.

Like all other birds, penguins lay eggs. Most penguins lay two eggs at a time, although sometimes only one chick is actually raised. Penguins have to keep the eggs warm until they hatch, and both parents usually share the job. When the chicks hatch about a month later, both parents help feed the young penguins. When the young penguins reach adult size, they shed their soft, fuzzy down and grow waterproof feathers. This is called *fledging*, and it is similar to something adult penguins do which is called *molting*. The adults drop their old feathers and grow stronger new ones that will help protect them against the freezing winds that come with winter.

A young penguin chick is covered in fuzzy down.

Except for the ones that live in zoos, all penguins live south of the equator. Some of them live on the icy continent of Antarctica. Other penguins live on islands off the coasts of South America, Africa, and Australia. Many penguins also hunt and nest on sub-Antarctic Islands, which are just north of Antarctica.

The Order of Living Things

A tiger has more in common with a house cat than it does with a daisy. A true bug is more like a butterfly than a jellyfish. Scientists arrange living things into groups based on how they look and how they act. A tiger and a house cat belong to the same group, but a daisy belongs to a different group.

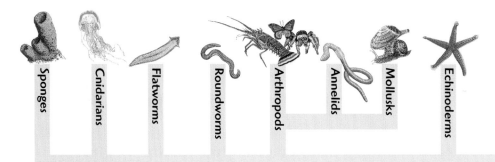

Sponges   Cnidarians   Flatworms   Roundworms   Arthropods   Annelids   Mollusks   Echinoderms

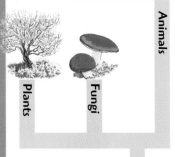

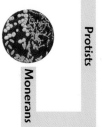

Animals

Plants   Fungi

Protists

Monerans

All living things can be placed in one of five groups called *kingdoms*: the plant kingdom, the animal kingdom, the fungus kingdom, the moneran kingdom, and the protist kingdom. You can probably name many of the creatures in the plant and animal kingdoms. The fungus kingdom includes mushrooms, yeasts, and molds. The moneran and protist kingdoms contain thousands of living things that are too small to see without a microscope.

8

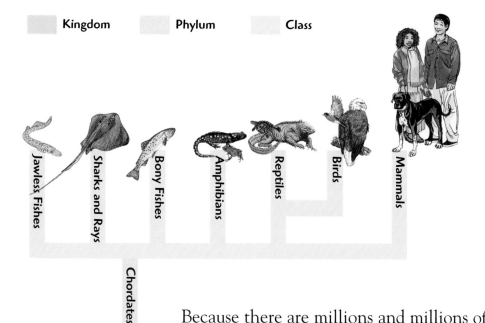

Kingdom   Phylum   Class

Jawless Fishes
Sharks and Rays
Bony Fishes
Amphibians
Reptiles
Birds
Mammals

Chordates

Because there are millions and millions of living things on Earth, some of the members of one kingdom may not seem all that similar. The animal kingdom includes creatures as different as tarantulas and trout, jellyfish and jaguars, salamanders and sparrows, and elephants and earthworms.

To show that an elephant is more like a jaguar than an earthworm, scientists further separate the creatures in each kingdom into more specific groups. The animal kingdom can be divided into nine *phyla.* Humans belong to the chordate phylum. Almost all chordates have a backbone.

Each phylum can be subdivided into many *classes.* Humans, mice, and elephants all belong to the mammal class. Each class can be further divided into orders; orders into *families,* families into *genera,* and genera into *species.* All the members of a species are very similar.

How the Sphenisciformes Fit In

You can probably guess that sphenisciformes belong to the animal kingdom. They have much more in common with spiders and snakes than they do with maple trees and morning glories.

Sphenisciformes are members of the chordate phylum. Most chordates have backbones and skeletons. Can you think of other chordates? Examples include elephants, mice, snakes, frogs, fish, whales, and humans.

All birds belong to the same class. There are about thirty orders of birds. Sphenisciformes make up one of these orders.

Scientists divide sphenisciformes into one family and six genera. There are seventeen species of sphenisciformes. They live on coasts and islands throughout the Southern Hemisphere. In this book you will learn more about fourteen species of sphenisciformes.

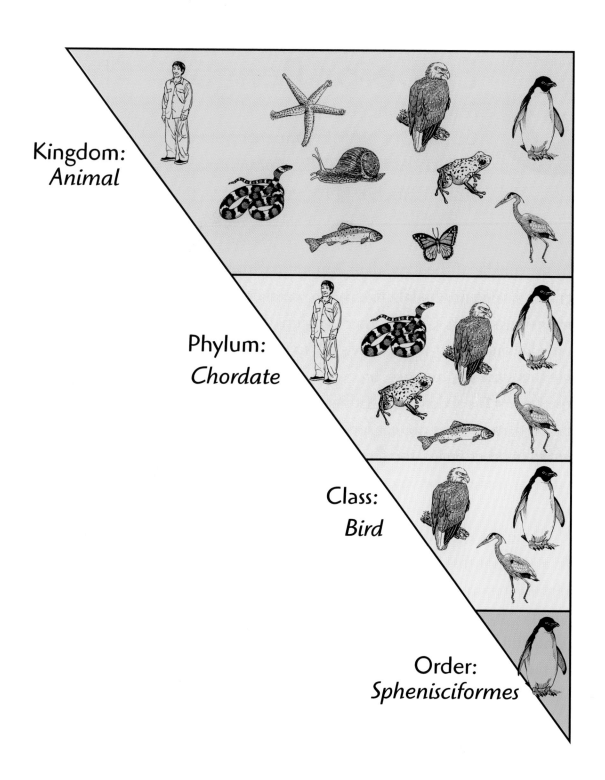

Kingdom:
Animal

Phylum:
Chordate

Class:
Bird

Order:
Sphenisciformes

Emperor Penguin

FAMILY: Spheniscidae
COMMON NAME: Emperor penguin
GENUS AND SPECIES: *Aptenodytes forsteri*
SIZE: 45 inches (115 cm)

In the middle of the long, dark Antarctic winter, large groups of male emperor penguins huddle together to keep both themselves and their mates' eggs warm. Unlike other penguins, female emperor penguins only lay one egg. It is the male's job to *incubate* the egg until it hatches. He tucks the egg into his "brood pouch," which is a small flap of skin at the base of his abdomen, right above his feet. The male cannot hunt for food, so he does not eat for two months. While he shuffles into a group of other males, the female treks the long way to the ocean. She will stay there for two months, eating and growing stronger. Then she returns to the nest, just in time for the egg to hatch.

Once the egg is hatched, both parents take turns raising the chick. In a few months, the chick is big enough to join a *crèche*. A crèche is like a penguin day-care center. It is a group of young penguins, usually watched by an adult, that gathers together to stay safe from the cold wind and hungry predators. By the end of summer, the chick has shed its fluffy down and grown adult feathers.

Emperor penguins are the largest penguins and the only ones that breed in the winter. They make their homes on the thick ice of the Antarctic continent, where their dense feathers, blubber, and slow

12

movements help keep them warm. Like all other penguins, they catch their food in the ocean. Emperor penguins usually dive about 165 feet (50 meters) down, but are able to dive up to 820 feet (250 m). They can remain underwater for up to eighteen minutes without coming to the surface for air.

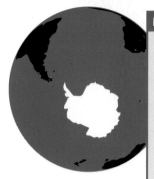

Adelie Penguin

FAMILY: Spheniscidae
COMMON NAME: Adelie penguin
GENUS AND SPECIES: *Pygoscelis adeliae*
SIZE: 27 1/2 inches (70 cm)

An adelie penguin zips through the ocean after krill. With a burst of speed, it shoots forward and snaps up a mouthful of the tiny creatures. After it has eaten, the penguin jumps straight up out of the water onto the shore, avoiding the sharp rocks at the water's edge. It waddles over to its pebble-lined nest and *regurgitates*, or throws up, some half-digested krill for its hungry chicks. The krill is now soft enough for the young penguins to gulp down easily.

Adelie penguins nest together in large, noisy *colonies* on the Antarctic continent and nearby islands. Females usually lay two eggs at a time, and both parents incubate them. The first egg that is laid hatches first, and that chick gets the most food from its parents. The second chick must wait for its older sibling to leave the nest before it can have its full share of tasty fish, squid, and krill.

Once their chicks are grown up, the parents leave the nesting grounds for the winter. They molt on ice floes and spend the winter hunting for food in the depths of the cold ocean. When they return to the breeding grounds in the spring, males raise their wings and call to their mates from the year before. Even in a huge, loud colony, a female penguin can recognize its mate's special call.

Adelie penguins have thick feathers to keep them warm in the freezing Antarctic winds. Their blubber protects them when they dive after their meals. If they have to, adelie penguins can live for a long time without eating. They survive on fat stored in their bodies while they search the ocean for fish or krill to eat.

Gentoo Penguin

FAMILY: *Spheniscidae*
COMMON NAME: Gentoo penguin
GENUS AND SPECIES: *Pygoscelis papua*
SIZE: 29–31 inches (75–81 cm)

It may be summer on the Antarctic *Peninsula*, but it's cold! A male gentoo penguin crouches over its two newborn chicks to keep them warm and safe from the chilly wind. Protected by their father and the round, pebble-lined nest, the hungry chicks wait for their mother to return with a tasty meal of half-digested fish. By autumn, the chicks will be big enough to catch their own food, but first they must grow strong, waterproof adult feathers. The soft down of newborn chicks could never keep them warm while diving for food in the cold ocean.

Similar to other penguins, gentoo penguins dive into the ocean to catch their meals. Their small, torpedo-shaped bodies are perfect for fast swimming. If they have to, gentoo penguins can swim up to 27 miles (45 km) an hour. As they speed through the water, they shoot above the surface every so often to get a breath of air. When a gentoo penguin hops out of the water onto shore, it can be very hot after swimming so fast. It stands still and raises its wings to cool off. It might look as though it is drying off, but it is not. Because of their waterproof feathers, penguins never really get wet.

Gentoo penguins live on the Antarctic Peninsula and throughout the sub-Antarctic islands. They spend the winter on the thick

16

Antarctic ice, diving for food in the freezing ocean. When spring arrives, they travel to beaches and bare hillsides to mate, lay their eggs, and raise their chicks. Once autumn comes, gentoo penguins molt on shore. They shed their old feathers and wait for dense new feathers to grow. Then they are ready once more for the long Antarctic winter.

King Penguin

FAMILY: Spheniscidae
COMMON NAME: King penguin
GENUS AND SPECIES: *Aptenodytes patagonicus*
SIZE: 36 inches (91 cm)

Whoosh! A king penguin slides across the ice on its large, round belly. It pushes off from the ice with its wings and lets the slippery surface slide it forward. This is called "tobogganing" because it is similar to a human sliding around on a toboggan. Since their bodies are so big and their legs are so short, "tobogganing" is the easiest way for king penguins to move quickly. At about 3 feet (1 m) tall, king penguins are the second-largest penguins in the world.

King penguins live mostly on sub-Antarctic islands, but often breed on the northern coast of Antarctica. They dive into the freezing ocean to catch juicy squid, small fish, and krill. Sometimes they must dive as deep as 165 feet (50 m) before they find food, and even deeper in the winter. King penguins often hunt in small groups, so that they can learn different hunting tricks from each other.

When spring comes, king penguins flock to the beaches and valleys to breed and raise chicks. Since it takes a chick a whole year to mature, king penguins can only breed twice in three years. They tend their chicks in colonies of penguins that can range in size from thirty penguins to tens of thousands of penguins. King penguin chicks are fed huge amounts of food to prepare them for the coming winter.

They grow quickly into large, fuzzy balls of down that are almost big enough to make their parents look small! With their thick down and large size, these chicks look almost like a different species of penguin. In fact, early explorers thought they *were* a different species. For a long time, king penguin chicks were known as "woolly penguins."

Macaroni Penguin

FAMILY: *Spheniscidae*
COMMON NAME: Macaroni penguin
GENUS AND SPECIES: *Eudyptes chrysolophus*
SIZE: 28 inches (71 cm)

How did macaroni penguins get their name? They may sound like some kind of pasta, but these penguins really have their feathers to thank for their name. When early English explorers first spotted macaroni penguins, they thought their vivid, orange head crests looked a lot like the feathery hats worn by certain fashionable men in England who were known as "macaronis." The explorers started calling the penguins "macaronis," and the name stuck.

Macaroni penguins make their homes throughout the sub-Antarctic islands. They pack themselves together into dense colonies high on rocky cliffs above the ocean. Sometimes the colonies contain more than one million penguins. With so many penguins in one place, the noise and smell can be extreme. If it is large enough, a colony of macaroni penguins can be smelled from up to 5 miles (8 km) offshore!

Female macaronis lay two eggs, but the first chick is often lost to a hungry sea bird, such as a skua or a petrel. Until the eggs hatch, both parents share the task of incubating them. After they hatch, however, it is the male penguin's job to guard the chicks while the female hunts for meals. She dives into the ocean for fish, squid, and

krill to carry back in her stomach for her chicks. She regurgitates the
half-digested food and the chicks gobble it down hungrily. After
about twenty-five days, the chicks are big enough to join a crèche of
other young penguins. By the time April or May comes, the chicks
have grown their adult feathers and are ready to catch their own
food in the chilly ocean.

Chinstrap Penguin

FAMILY: Spheniscidae
COMMON NAME: Chinstrap penguin
GENUS AND SPECIES: *Pygoscelis antarctica*
SIZE: 26–30 inches (68–77 cm)

That was a close call! A chinstrap penguin jumps straight up onto the shore, narrowly escaping the jaws of a hungry leopard seal. It is high noon, the perfect feeding time for chinstrap penguins and therefore the perfect feeding time for leopard seals. Penguins have to be careful when diving into the ocean in search of the fish and krill they love to eat. There are plenty of predators on the lookout for a bite of tasty penguin.

Chinstrap penguins get their name from the thin black band of feathers under their chins. Even in a crowd of similar-looking gentoos and adelies, you can always spot this penguin by looking for its "chinstrap." Chinstraps live on the Antarctic Peninsula and throughout the sub-Antarctic islands. In the summer, they live and breed in large colonies on rough, rocky slopes, often near gentoo and adelie penguins. In the winter, they move onto pack ice and often can be found on huge icebergs in the open ocean. Chinstrap penguins are good at moving around on jagged ice and rocks. They climb using all their limbs and jump long distances to get from one rock to another. When they want to move fast, they "toboggan" across the ice, sliding on their bellies and pushing with their wings.

Female chinstrap penguins lay two eggs at a time in round nests lined with pebbles. Both parents take turns keeping the eggs warm until they hatch. The newly hatched chicks are small, downy, and helpless at first, but they grow quickly. After about two months, the chicks shed their soft down and grow strong adult feathers that will keep them warm while they dive for food. By the time winter rolls around, the chicks are skilled at swimming underwater after delicious fish and krill.

Galapagos Penguin

FAMILY: Spheniscidae
COMMON NAME: Galapagos penguin
GENUS AND SPECIES: *Spheniscus mendiculus*
SIZE: 19–21 inches (48–53 cm)

A Galapagos penguin spends the day swimming in the ocean, gobbling up sardines and mullet. Its thick feathers keep it warm in the chilly ocean currents that flow through its home in the Galapagos Islands. When it hops back onto land, however, the bright sun can make this penguin very hot. To battle the heat, Galapagos penguins pant like dogs or lift their feathers up to let the cool breezes reach their skin. Because it can be so warm on land, these penguins usually spend all day in the ocean. They only scramble onto shore when night comes and cools down the islands.

Galapagos penguins live solely on the Galapagos Islands, a cluster of rocky islands just south of the equator in the Pacific Ocean. Unlike the penguins in the Antarctic, these penguins live alone with their mates or in small groups of about two or three pairs. They stay in the same place during both winter and summer and can breed at any time of the year. In fact, if there is enough food to go around, a female can lay up to three clutches of eggs a year. This has helped rebuild their population after periods when there were not enough sardines or mullet to feed the hungry penguins and many died. Galapagos penguins usually mate for life, which helps them lay eggs more

often. They build their nests in caves or crevices that have formed in old, hardened lava.

Because they are so small, Galapagos penguins have a lot of enemies. In the ocean, they have to watch out for sharks, seals, and sea lions. On land, they protect their eggs and chicks from hungry hawks that are on the prowl. Sometimes even the domestic dogs and cats people have brought to the islands will snatch Galapagos penguin chicks from their nests.

Humboldt Penguin

FAMILY: Spheniscidae
COMMON NAMES: Humboldt penguin,
   Peruvian penguin
GENUS AND SPECIES: *Spheniscus humboldti*
SIZE: 17 inches (60 cm)

Letting a refreshing breeze blow through its feathers, a Humboldt penguin sits in the shade to cool off. It is hot after swimming through the ocean, chasing tasty anchovies and sardines. With their dense feathers and thick skin, these penguins can heat up quickly in the warm sun. Sometimes a Humboldt penguin will open its mouth and pant to keep itself from overheating. Their feathers keep them cozy and dry in the ocean, however, where a certain ocean current called the Humboldt current can make the water very chilly.

Humboldt penguins live together in small, friendly groups off the coasts of Peru and Chile. They nest with their family and friends in caves close to sea level, where it is only a short hop to the ocean. These penguins used to nest in large, hardened piles of *guano*, which are droppings left by sea birds. However, people started collecting the guano when they realized it made very good fertilizer. Now there is not enough guano left for penguins to dig their nests in, so they make do with caves. The caves help keep their eggs and chicks safe from hungry gulls and skuas.

A female Humboldt penguin can lay eggs any time during the

year. First, the male picks out a good place for the nest. Then, he courts the female by bowing and bobbing his head. If the female likes him, the pair usually will mate for life. The female lays two eggs, and both parents help keep them warm. Once the chicks hatch, the two adults are kept very busy. Sometimes they will travel up to 45 miles (75 km) in one day to find enough fish to feed their chicks. They dive into the water after schools of sardines and anchovies. Then they swim back to their nests and cough up the half-digested fish for their hungry chicks. The chicks grow quickly, and after about three months, they are ready for life on their own.

Magellanic Penguin
FAMILY: Spheniscidae
COMMON NAMES: Magellanic penguin
GENUS AND SPECIES: *Spheniscus magellanicus*
SIZE: 17 inches (60 cm)

What kind of penguin lives on sandy ground? Magellanic penguins do. Millions of these noisy penguins make their homes in the deserts on the Punta Tombo Peninsula, a nature preserve on the coast of Patagonia. They scratch their nests into the sandy soil, usually under shrubs that will help protect their chicks from hungry gulls. When they're not keeping their eggs and chicks warm, Magellanic penguins are hunting for squid and small fish in the nearby ocean. Once they catch something, they hop out of the water and waddle back across the dusty desert to feed their peeping chicks.

Magellanic penguins also nest on grassy slopes and in open woodland, any place where their eggs will be safe from predators. They live mostly on the coast of Patagonia in Argentina, but also along the coast of Chile. Some Magellanic penguins make their homes on the warmer sub-Antarctic islands. They return to their breeding grounds around September, which is the beginning of the South American spring. After they raise their chicks, they shed their old feathers and grow stronger ones. Then they travel north-ward for the winter.

Similar to other penguins, these penguins like to crowd together

in large, friendly colonies. The breeding colony at Punta Tombo contains up to one million penguins. That's a lot of penguins, especially when they're making a lot of noise! It's easy to hear a colony of Magellanic penguins. They make a variety of different sounds, from braying like donkeys to bleating and cackling. Each sound means something different, but only a Magellanic penguin really knows what another penguin is saying.

Rockhopper Penguin

FAMILY: Spheniscidae
COMMON NAME: Rockhopper penguin
GENUS AND SPECIES: *Eudyptes chrysocome*
SIZE: 21–24 inches (55–62 cm)

A group of rockhopper penguins jumps in single file up a steep cliff near the ocean. True to their name, they hop easily from one rock to another. When they reach extra steep parts, they latch their beaks onto the rocks. To keep from falling, they dig into the cliff with their toes. These penguins have just caught bellyfuls of fish in the ocean. They are on their way to feed their hungry chicks nesting at the tops of the cliffs. Rockhopper penguins build their nests high on sea cliffs. The deep caves and overhangs keep their babies safe from fierce gulls and skuas. After their chicks hatch, the adult penguins will hop up and down the cliffs many times a day to bring food to their young.

Rockhopper penguins are some of the most brightly colored penguins in the Falkland Islands and other islands near the coast of South America. They have bright red eyes, orange beaks, and colorful tufts of feathers that sprout from their heads. Unlike other penguins, they rarely waddle when they move. Instead, they hop with both feet together. It is the easiest way for a rockhopper penguin to get around on the jagged rocks of its island home.

Baby rockhoppers hatch around November. They spend about three weeks in their cozy, safe nests before they join crèches with

other young penguins. By the time they grow their adult feathers in March, it is almost time for the South American winter to start. The young penguins dive into the sea in search of tasty squid, fish, and other small creatures that will fatten them up for the cold season. Even though they are large enough at this point to be safe from hungry gulls, these penguins still have to watch out for other predators. Sharks and seals are always cruising the ocean, hoping to snag an unlucky penguin or two.

Little Penguin

FAMILY: Spheniscidae
COMMON NAMES: Little penguin, Fairy penguin, Little blue penguin
GENUS AND SPECIES: *Eudyptula minor*
SIZE: 15–17 inches (40–45 cm)

It is early evening on the southern Australian coast. A crowd of little penguins is waddling quickly up the beach. These small penguins have spent the whole day in the ocean, diving underwater to catch fish, octopuses, squid, and tiny *crustaceans*. With their bellies full of food, they are on their way back home to their nests. Nestled in underground burrows, their chicks peep hungrily as they wait for their parents to arrive.

Standing only 15 inches (40 cm) tall, little penguins are the smallest penguins in the world. They get their name from their small size, but they also are called "fairy penguins" or "little blue penguins." They live mostly on the coasts of southern Australia and Tasmania, but will sometimes nest in New Zealand or on sub-Antarctic islands. During the daytime, they guard their nests or hunt in the ocean. These penguins find most of their meals in the top 16 or 17 feet (5 m) of water, but they can dive up to 226 feet (69 m) down if they have to. When a little penguin spots a school of fish, it plunges straight into the middle and grabs a single fish in its bill. It gulps it down and glides back to the water's surface smoothly.

Little penguins make many different sounds. They bray loudly to declare their territory, bark to each other while hunting in the sea, and croon softly when returning to their nests at night. When a male wants to find a mate, he points his head and flippers upward and brays loudly. If a female likes him, they dig an underground burrow together in which she lays two eggs. Sometimes little penguins will even nest under buildings, between the ties of railway tracks, or in stacks of lumber.

Yellow-eyed Penguin

FAMILY: Spheniscidae
COMMON NAME: Yellow-eyed penguin
GENUS AND SPECIES: *Megadyptes antipodes*
SIZE: 21 inches (65 cm)

While their parents are off hunting for meals, two yellow-eyed penguin chicks snuggle together in their warm nest. They peep with hunger, waiting for their parents to return with cod or arrow squid. The chicks are alone because yellow-eyed penguins build their nests far away from other penguins. They like to live in forests or on grassy slopes near the ocean—anywhere that is private.

These shy penguins make their homes on the islands south of New Zealand, including Auckland, Campbell, Stewart, and South Islands. They dive for food by themselves or in small groups of two or three other penguins. The beginning of the breeding season in August is a busy time. This is one of the few times they gather in large groups. The males show off, flashing the yellow stripes on their heads and bowing to the females. Once a couple gets together, though, they disappear into the forest to raise their chicks. Although they remain in a loose colony, they build their nests far apart. They will not gather in a large group until it is time for them to molt again in March. They cannot hunt for food while they are molting, and afterward they are skinny and hungry. They dive into the ocean, snapping up cod, silversides, opal fish, and squid.

You can recognize yellow-eyed penguins easily by their bright yellow eyes and the yellow stripe that curves over their heads. They may be the fourth-largest penguin in the world, but they still have to watch out for enemies. Hungry seals chase them in the ocean and domestic dogs sometimes attack them on land. Parents also have to guard their eggs and chicks from ferrets and wildcats.

Erect-crested Penguin

FAMILY: Spheniscidae
COMMON NAME: Erect-crested penguin
GENUS AND SPECIES: *Eudyptes sclateri*
SIZE: 25–27 inches (63–68 cm)

It is September, the beginning of the penguin breeding season in the Antipodes Islands. Two male erect-crested penguins fight fiercely over a nesting site. They knock their bills together and snap at each other, growling deeply. On these small, crowded islands, good nesting places are rare. Once the female penguins arrive, the males greet their mates with steady, harsh calls. The reunited couples build small nests out of stones and mud. Then the female lays two eggs, although only one of them hatches usually.

Two stiff, yellow crests sprout from the heads of these well-named penguins. They swing these crests back and forth when they want to tell other penguins, "Go away." This is very useful on the crowded islands. When the winter ends, erect-crested penguins gather together in large colonies on the rocky island coasts south of New Zealand. They nest on beaches or on flat rock platforms at the tops of the cliffs. Once their eggs hatch, the parents must climb up the cliffs with their stomachs full of freshly caught fish or squid. They regurgitate the food for their young, who gobble it up hungrily.

Erect-crested penguins go on huge eating sprees as soon as their

36

babies have grown up. Soon they will molt, losing all their feathers before growing stronger ones. These penguins have to eat all they can before they molt.

African Penguin

FAMILY: Spheniscidae
COMMON NAMES: African penguin,
   Jackass penguin, Black-footed penguin
GENUS AND SPECIES: *Spheniscus demersus*
SIZE: 17 inches (60 cm)

"Hee haw!" Is that a donkey? No, it's an African penguin, braying loudly to tell other penguins, "This is my home." Because their loud voices sound so similar to the braying of donkeys, African penguins are sometimes called "jackass penguins." "Jackass" is another word for a donkey. Sometimes they use a different call to keep in touch with each other while swimming. Other times they squawk when startled or croon softly to their chicks when bringing them food.

African penguins are the only kind of penguin that lives near Africa. They hunt and breed year-round on the islands off the southern African coast, where the ocean is cool enough for their dense feathers and thick blubber. African penguins dive into the water to catch sardines, anchovies, and squid. They stay in the ocean most of the day to avoid the hot African sun. When they scramble ashore, bare patches on their flippers and feet help them let the heat out of their bodies. Sometimes they open their beaks and pant like dogs to cool down.

When two mates are raising chicks, they like to be by them-

selves most of the time. They scratch a small nest under rocks or bushes, and the female lays two eggs. African penguins used to dig their nests in guano, but humans collected most of it for fertilizer. Now these penguins have to make do with what they have. Bushes don't provide much shelter from enemies, though. Hungry gulls and wildcats carry off a lot of African penguin chicks each year. The chicks that survive grow quickly, however. By the time they are three months old, they are ready to dive into the ocean after their own anchovies and sardines.

Penguins and People

You may be surprised to learn that people have changed the lives of many kinds of penguins over the years. Some people used to hunt penguins for food or for their skins, but very few people hunt penguins anymore. Sometimes people collect penguin eggs to eat, but that is not as popular anymore either. Other times people harm penguins by taking the things they need, like food or places to build nests. Much of the time, however, people do not even know that their actions hurt penguins.

Some penguins live quite happily near humans. Little penguins in Australia do not seem to mind people. They even build their nests under people's houses, if they cannot find a better spot. It may sound fun to have penguins living under your house, but nesting penguins can be pretty noisy! Between the peeping of hungry chicks

Little penguins are comfortable living very close to humans.

and the braying of their parents, people may wish the penguins would just go away.

Other run-ins between humans and penguins are not so friendly. Ever since people discovered that guano (bat droppings) makes great fertilizer, they have been collecting it off the coastal rocks of South America and Africa. This causes a big problem for Humboldt and African penguins, which both used to dig small burrows in the guano to use as nests. Without the hard shell of guano to keep their eggs safe, these penguins have been losing more of their young to hungry predators. They build their nests under bushes or rock ledges, but there are not enough of these resting sites for all of the birds and the penguins fight over them fiercely.

Sometimes people and penguins fight over the same kinds of food. Fishermen catch some of the same fish species that penguins eat. The large anchovy fishing industry off the coasts of Peru and Chile makes it hard for Humboldt penguins to find enough fish to eat. The fishing of sardines, krill, and other marine creatures threatens the food supply of other kinds of penguins across the world.

Penguins can get tangled in fishing nets or in rubbish left by fishermen and tourists who visit penguin colonies. If they are left tangled for too long, they will die of starvation. Penguins are also in big danger from oil spills. If ships clean out their tanks near a penguin colony or spill their cargo by mistake, the oil clogs the penguins' feathers and kills the fish in the ocean. Many penguins have died from oil spills.

Even the penguins that live far away from people have problems. Penguins that live in Antarctica may be harmed from

Global warming may cause the ice in Antartica to melt.

global warming. Humans create pollution that eats away at the *ozone layer* in the atmosphere. This destroys the Earth's natural protection from the burning rays of the sun. Since the ozone layer has thinned, temperatures in some places have increased. If it keeps getting hotter, the ice in Antarctica may start to melt.

In an effort to protect penguins, some governments have created national parks or wildlife preserves out of the land where penguins nest. This helps keep them safe from hunters and fishermen. People try to keep predators such as seals, wildcats, and domestic dogs away from penguins. They hope that if they give the penguins a chance to survive, they will lay more eggs and their numbers will increase.

There are also organizations that rescue penguins from oil spills

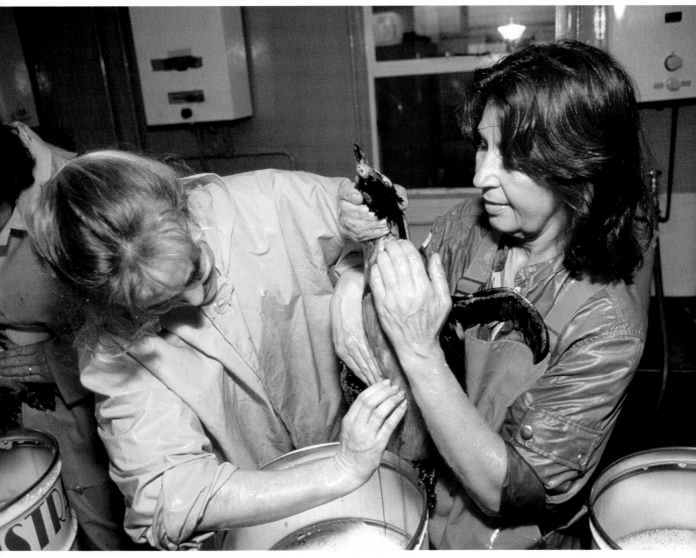

Rescue workers clean the oil from a penguin's feathers.

and clean their oil-clogged feathers. When the penguins are healthy again, the workers bring them back to their colonies. Some people protect penguins by providing boxes in which penguins can lay their eggs. Then the penguins do not have to fight over nesting sites, and their chicks have a better chance of growing up healthy.

Words to Know

camouflage—a device that disguises an object or creature to help it blend with its surroundings.

class—a group of creatures within a phylum that share certain characteristics.

colony—a large group of animals, such as birds, that live and nest together.

crèche—a group of young penguins that stay together for protection from predators and harsh weather.

crustacean—an arthropod with several pairs of jointed legs, a hard outer shell, two pairs of antennae, and eyes at the ends of stalks. Lobsters, crabs, shrimps, and crayfish are all crustaceans.

excrete—to expel waste from the body.

family—a group of creatures within an order that share certain characteristics.

fledging—growing adult wing and tail feathers.

genus (plural **genera**)—a group of creatures within a family that share certain characteristics.

guano—the droppings of certain animals, such as birds and bats.

incubate—to keep an egg warm until it hatches.

kingdom—one of the five categories into which all living things are placed: the animal kingdom, the plant kingdom, the fungus kingdom, the moneran kingdom, and the protist kingdom.

molting—shedding old feathers in order to replace them with new ones.

ozone layer—the layer of the upper atmosphere that absorbs harmful ultraviolet radiation from the sun.

peninsula—an area of land that is bordered on three sides by water.

phylum (plural **phyla**)—a group of creatures within a kingdom that share certain characteristics.

species—a group of creatures within a genus that share certain characteristics. Members of the same species can mate and produce young.

regurgitate—to bring undigested or partially digested food up from the stomach to the mouth, as some birds and animals do to feed their young.

Learning More

Books

Davis, Lloyd Spencer. *Penguin: A Season in the Life of the Adelie Penguin*. New York: Harcourt Brace & Co., 1994.

Hodge, Judith. *Penguins (Animals of the Oceans)*. New York: Barrows Juveniles, 1999.

Peterson, Roger Tory. *Penguins*. Boston: Houghton Mifflin, 1998.

Robinson, Claire. *Penguins (In the Wild)*. New York: Heinemann Library, 2001.

Schafer, Kevin. *Penguin Planet: Their World, Our World*. New York: Creative Publishing International, 2000.

Videos

World of Penguins. Educational Broadcasting Corporation.

Mother Nature Tales of Discovery: Penguins in Paradise. Discovery Communications.

Internet Sites

Pete and Barb's Penguin Pages
http://ourworld.compuserve.com/homepages/Pete
This sites provides information on all seventeen species of penguin, including facts, pictures, and where to find them in zoos and aquariums around the world.

Bird-Watching in Antarctica
http://www.geocities.com/Yosemite/Gorge/5404/
This site offers facts and pictures of penguins, as well as other animals of the Antarctic.

Index

About the Author

Erin Pembrey Swan studied animal behavior, literature, and early childhood education at Hampshire College in Massachusetts. She also studied literature and history at University College, Galway, in Ireland and creative writing at New School University in Manhattan. Her poetry has been published in various journals, both in the United States and Ireland. Ms. Swan has written seven other books in the Animals in Order series, including *Primates: From Howler Monkeys to Humans*, *Land Predators of North America*, *Kangaroos and Koalas: What They Have in Common*, and *Pelicans, Cormorants, and Their Kin*. She is also the author of *India*, a book in the Enchantment of the World series. Ms. Swan currently lives and works in New York City.